Go HARD or Go Home!

Pastor Lyddale J. Akins

Go HARD or Go Home!

Published by Kingdom Publishing, LLC
www.kingdompublishingllc.com

Printed in the United States of America 2019—First Edition

Copyright © 2019 by Lyddale J. Akins

All rights reserved. Except as permitted under the U.S. Copyright Act of 1976, this publication shall not be broadcast, rewritten, distributed, or transmitted, electronically or copied, in any form, or stored in a database or retrieval system, without prior written permission from the author.

ISBN 9781947741430

1. Akins, Lyddale 2. Spiritual Growth 3. Personal Growth
4. Relationship Growth 5. Christianity

Unless otherwise indicated, Scripture quotations are taken from the King James Version (KJV) (public domain). Scripture quotations marked (NIV) are taken from the Holy Bible, New International Version®, NIV®. Copyright © 1973, 1978, 1984 by Biblica, Inc.™ Used by permission of Zondervan. All rights reserved worldwide. http://www.zondervan.com. Scripture quotations marked (AMP) are taken from the Amplified® Bible. Copyright © 1954, 1958, 1962, 1964, 1965, 1987 by The Lockman Foundation. Used by permission. www.Lockman.org

Akins Ministry
500 Malterer Avenue, Oceanport NJ 07757
www.relationshipsuniversity.com

TABLE OF CONTENTS

INTRODUCTION..1

SECTION ONE: Relationship with God........................9
What Am I Here For?..10
Deeper into PURPOSE..12
ALL I NEED IS ONE...15
Matters of the Soul...19
You are Not the OWNER!..32
The Breaking Process..34
The Water Process..36
Sanctification...39

SECTION TWO: Relationship with Yourself..............41
Seize the Day..42
Pluck the Day...44
Living a FULL Life..47
I Am My Worst Enemy!..49
The Pain of Loss..51
The Outcome of Pain...53
The Process of Pain..56

SECTION THREE: Relationship with People...............59
Real Fulfillment...63
Encourage Yourself..66
Fear Factor..69
The Bigger Picture..72
F.E.A.R. Defined...76
What's Love Got to Do With It?..79
Love According to 1 Corinthians 13..................................81
Make A Change Now!..86

ACKNOWLEDGEMENTS..89

INTRODUCTION

On February 2, 2006 my life changed in a drastic way. I went from mediocrity to destiny. I went from regular faith to radical faith. In moments, everything changed. It all began when I decided to launch the House of Prayer at the West Side Community Center. My first prospects were a few friends and students from my wife's school, totaling twenty people. I was so excited! I could barely keep myself calm. My wife and I cleaned, painted, and transformed the room into something like a sanctuary. Every Thursday, we would set up and break down. We would restack the toilet paper, prepare the napkins, place fabric across the tables, vacuum the carpet, put the chairs out and position the pulpit. We did this faithfully for two months, but it wasn't growing like I thought it would.

I'd be lying if I said I didn't question God during this process.

The next month, a young man was shot outside the building right in front of the gate. What a devastating blow to the ministry! Due to safety concerns, over half of the people left. They felt the neighborhood wasn't a good "fit" for them and they told us to our faces that God had called me into this, but not them! Heavy punch to my spirit! Sometimes it felt like a literal punch to the body. I was frustrated and shocked. I can even admit that I was disappointed. I knew what God had told me to do, yet everything appeared to be going in the opposite direction. I mean really.

I left a job that was paying me $40,000/year with benefits. I left on nothing but faith. And here was the real kicker: I never gave up even though it got darker and darker. Instead of throwing in the towel, I decided to "Go Hard." Instead of giving in to my discouragement, I told the remaining members to get ready for a mind-blowing launch Service on April 16, 2006. I planned for the greatest program ever! I asked the lady who ran the community center to reserve the gymnasium, equipped with a stage and 150-300 chairs. I set out as many chairs as I could.

I'm going to fill this place up, I thought to myself.

Well, indeed it was an awesome EASTER CELEBRATION service! There were 150 chairs set up and about seven people came. Did you hear me? Seven people! But you couldn't have told me anything! I preached that day like I was preaching to a stadium with thousands of listeners. I forgot to mention: two of the people were my cousin and her friend who drove two hours from Long Island (NY) to Asbury Park (NJ) to support us.

Yes. That's right. They skipped their own service that day at Perfecting Faith Church with Pastor Donnie McClurkin, and I'm sure they were shocked to see the turnout. *Can you say with me DISCOURAGED!* But I didn't give in to my feelings. Instead, I decided to GO HARD!

Each person who attended the launch service that day caused my faith to increase. They pushed me to intensify my prayer and devotional time with God. That was the moment that my life began to change. Why?

Because I was learning, through experience, how to trust what God said, even though I couldn't see any evidence.

I developed tougher skin. I learned to lean on God in a totally different way. I told the Lord that day, "I will go as hard as I can to build what You told me to build." I wasn't willing to give up on this dream, especially because I knew that God had called me to reach my destiny. So, for financial reasons we switched the church to our home. I printed post cards and passed out thousands of flyers. I talked and talked and talked until we began to see growth. My family began coming and other families started to pile in until we could no longer fit in my house. I then started to pray and ask God for the next step.

We were now at about 30 people. The time was right to move out of my house; especially when people began to drive by and just ring the doorbell and just walk in without my knowledge! I recall a lady who said she was driving by and stopped in while we were praising God. She said, "I felt like God wanted me to come in here and just experience His presence." At that point, I knew it was time to think beyond the confines of my home. I prayed for a location, and trusted God to meet me at the point of my faith.

It was now around September of 2006. God opened up the door for us to house our services in a free space! It was 800 square feet with a bathroom at a shopping center. If I had become caught up in the look of it or the size of it, I would've missed my blessing. But something about this property told me that it was a blessing from God. The owner normally gave it out to people running for political office, but he said we were welcome to use it for our purposes. I was blown away by God's favor, and I was ready to sign the dotted line. But within two months, God did something else! Another door opened on December 24, 2006, allowing us to move into our Triumphant Life Church facility. God fast tracked us because we pushed beyond disappointment and fear. We walked into a 6000 square foot building. It was fully renovated and had everything we needed. But that is not all!

We grew to 100 people within a 90-day period. Things started happening very quickly. I "randomly" met a guy at a wedding, and the next thing I know, he recommended me to become the pastor of an Assembly of God church. He said I was the perfect person to take over their ministry because a lot of his people had been hurt, abandoned and needed love. But that wasn't all! God began to build my confidence and strengthen my preaching ability. I realized very quickly how God will fast track you if you stay focused and faithful about your future.

Not before long, more and more people began to notice what we were doing. Just think what would've happened if I had given up too soon. Just imagine the people that might not be in church today if my wife and I had resigned to the situation in front of us. It was during a tough transition in life that my entire perspective changed. Donations were coming in from left and right, and we were well on our way to becoming a thriving church plant…all because I was determined to GO HARD!

GO H.A.R.D. DEFINED!

What does the term "go h.a.r.d" mean? *I'm so glad you asked.* On the one hand, "going hard" could mean different things to different people. In today's generation, for example, we have a popular saying, "Go Hard or Go Home!" Go Hard or Go Home implies that a person should give 100% of themselves, or else they might as well not try. To "Go HARD" is to go all out at whatever you are doing at that time. To "go hard" means to give it your all! In many cases, it's the one who is bold and brave; and particularly the one who will push beyond the norm that will earn this label of going hard.

Many people Go Hard for things they want, but they neglect the things they need. I've witnessed people buy what they want and beg for what they need. For example, many people beg for love, but will buy a closet full of clothes to mask their loneliness. Many people will beg for a family, but instead of going after what they need, they will settle for fickle friends. When people beg for something, it is not based on class or status. Any social group might find themselves going after what they think they want and neglecting what they truly need.

Our nation as a whole tends to skip the things we need in order to choose the easier road. We would rather have dessert than to live a life of destiny. This book, however, is written with those in mind who are determined to go hard or go home.

INTRODUCTION

Now let me explain what it means to "go home." In our society, home is where the heart is. Home is a place of comfort. For many people, it is the place of stagnancy. When people are home, they don't work. They sleep. They eat. They are cozy and warm snuggled next to their loved ones on the couch watching television. But life is not supposed to be con- fined to your home! God has more for you outside of your comfort zone. Don't get so consumed with feeding the kids, playing video games, and paying bills that you forget that God has greater in store for you! *Home is a great place but if you never leave your home, you will never earn a living! You will never meet divine connections, and you will never grow.*

I said all of that to say this: I hope you are ready to walk down a life-changing path that will get you to a place of destiny. I will define this term "destiny" in the chapters to come, but for now, let me admit this fact: each one of us has a predetermined path that God has designed for us. If we follow His plan and design for our lives, we will reap much success. The Bible reminds us in Jeremiah 29:11-For I know the plans I have for you," says the Lord. "They are plans for good and not for disaster, to give you a future and a hope. God has a plan for you and this plan is not a puzzle, it is a platter. The platter means He will serve you the nutrients necessary for you to grow. He doesn't make life difficult. We make it harder than we have to all because most of us haven't separated our needs from our wants. But if you go to God, then you will experience the goods of life. If you go to God, then you can grow past your emotional failures and experience mental success. If we are going to get to the plans that God has for us, then we must concentrate and meditate on the Word as frequently as possible. It is imperative that you complete this book at this moment in your life because your next season depends on it. You cannot lose focus during this moment in your life. You cannot waste your life doing just anything; because if you do, it will cost you everything. It will cost you time, energy and money.

Take this journey with me through three central aspects of life that are important to examine: your relationship with God, your relationship with yourself, and your relationship with people. Each category has various sublevels that will range from topics like fear, money, health, love, success, focus, and faith—but trust me, the words in each chapter are equipped to strengthen you and to enable you.

My primary message is simple, so if you don't remember anything else in this introduction, remember this: you have a destiny; and that destiny is reachable. But in order to achieve it, you must go hard! You must be determined. You must be willing to have your plans changed. You must be honest with yourself, and most of all, you must have a relationship with God. The acronym Go H.A.R.D. stands for Helping Access Reachable Destiny, and it is my prayer that through this book you will receive a powerful tool to help you reach and exceed your God-given destiny. Get ready for the greatest years of your life!

SECTION ONE
RELATIONSHIP WITH GOD

Chapter 1
What Am I Here For?

There has never been and will never be anyone like you. You have a unique destiny and a special purpose. You have something to do in this life that God intends you to do, and only you can accomplish it. Nobody can steal it from you, and nobody can do it for you. So why do you do continue to go to work or school and live your life as if there is nothing more that you were designed to do? Why do you settle for less than the best? Why do you let others label you and restrict your life?

Let me share something with you. Your future depends on your understanding of destiny and purpose. These two words, when lived out, will cause passion for life, power to get through circumstances and they will produce favor in your life.

People often fail to recognize the difference between purpose and destiny. They use the terms interchangeably, as if they were identical or equivalent thoughts. But the two words are different, though they are related. Many people are living by accident, because they are not sure of their destiny or purpose.

Here is a simple way to think about it. Destiny should drive purpose, but if you don't know either, then you are just going through life with a haphazard mindset instead of with a GO HARD mindset. Those who live hard and go hard and work hard and pray hard, these folks know what they should be doing. They live life on purpose. Every conversation is intentional. Everything they do produces fruit. Why? Because purpose drives action. Purpose will cause you to wake up and handle life differently. Purpose helps us by providing short-term focus for day-to-day living. It allows you to wake up and pray. It inspires you to read your Word, it causes you to want to be around other people, and to serve God with your life. However, destiny will provide the long-term perspective and direction you need to win in life. When I understand my destiny, I don't let temporary situations disturb my permanent direction in life. I don't let temporary people become permanent stumbling blocks. When I understand my destiny, I don't build a house on tent-like soil.

Chapter 2
Deeper into PURPOSE

Several writers have penned awesome books on purpose and destiny, but many people have yet to realize their true purpose and destiny. Rick Warren, a best selling Christian author and mega church pastor, wrote a wonderful book called *PURPOSE DRIVEN LIFE*, which directs us to five areas that God created us for:

Purpose #1: You Were Planned for God's Pleasure
       (Worship)

Purpose #2: You Were Formed for God's Family
       (Fellowship)

Purpose #3: You Were Created to Become Like Christ
       (Discipleship)

Purpose #4: You Were Shaped for Serving God
       (Ministry)

Purpose #5: You Were Made for a Mission
       (Mission)

I believe Rick Warren gives us a great blue print to stand on as it relates to purpose. Warren's book will help guide you on a day-to-day basis. However, we must be clear on destiny because it's going to give us perspective. Destiny provides direction for long-term success. Therefore, we need the right perspective if we are ever going to prevail in life. Why? Because perspective causes balance in your life. Perspective will cause you to reach your fullest potential and will bring you directly into your destiny.

My life is filled with examples of purpose kissing destiny. I now see the fruits of my decisions because I serve as a pastor to one of the greatest churches in the world. But that wasn't my previous plan. Imagine if I had never left the computer field and remained an engineer. Imagine if I had never become a youth pastor and instead, I accepted my first job offer in Trenton, NJ as a correction officer? Imagine if I had never gotten married. What if I had decided to stay single? How different might my life be if it weren't for certain destiny moves in my life?

You see, here is the thing about destiny. We never see destiny's full direction until we look in the rearview mirror of purpose. Until we see the purpose in it, we will never understand the destiny behind it. The two words work hand-in-hand. It was purpose that caused me to choose a youth pastor job, but destiny was that spiritual gift that gave me perspective about my decision. When it came time for me to resign as a youth pastor, it was the most difficult thing I had ever done. I loved serving as a youth pastor, but God was tugging on my heart for more. I would be lying if I said I had no reservations. But I kept giving God testers. I kept asking God to show me signs, but even when I didn't see the sign I heard His voice say, "I am with you." Each step I made, God showed up with favor in His hand. The harder I pushed, the greater and more visible God's hand became in my situation. And the same is true for you. God will never leave you by yourself. He will never give you gifts to accomplish something without also providing the plan to make sure it happens successfully. God is rooting for you more than you are rooting for yourself. His purpose in you is to do good and to bless those around you. The destiny on your life is too costly to give in to the temptation of mediocrity.

Romans 8:28 (NKJV) And we know that all things work together for good to those who love God, to those who are called according to His purpose.

All that we do is mapped out. God wants you to prosper and also to enjoy the journey. So, go back to my story for a moment. Sure, I could have worked as a correction officer, went to church and become an auxiliary leader in the church, but I would have been operating outside of my destiny. God's predesigned image of me was to pastor. It was impossible to achieve destiny without purpose, but also, I couldn't have been able to understand my short-term purpose without knowing my long-term destiny.

Chapter 3
ALL I NEED IS ONE

In the last chapter, we discussed the difference between destiny and purpose. In short, you need destiny because they are the tires on your vehicle that will keep your car afloat. Purpose, however, is equally as important because they are like the brakes on your car. If there were no brakes on your vehicle, you wouldn't drive out of your parking lot. Why? Because nobody (who is sane) would put themselves and others in danger.

Sometimes you've got to just slow down long enough and pay attention to the purpose behind the wheel. Nothing just happens. Pay attention to every little moment, because until you do, God cannot fully reveal to you what plans He has in line for your life. All you need is one moment of change, and one introduction to the right person, the right place, and the right perspective.

Bishop I.V. Hilliard believes this (and I agree with him): *"our standard for life is set by four factors: Environment, Others, Experiences and Repetitious Information. When considering your life, have you ever slowed down long enough to ask yourself these questions:*

Where am I spending my time?
Who am I with all the time?
Do they help me or hinder me?

Am I allowing my past to hinder my future?
Can I see myself beyond my current experiences?

The questions above will help you to see where purpose has taken a wrong turn in your life. Answering the questions will cause destiny to reroute your life like the GPS system in the car after a missed exit. Let's think about these four areas for a moment.

Places- They say, "birds of a feather, flock together." And in many ways, this statement is true. You are what you eat, but you become what you hang around. If you want to become smarter, go to school. Why? Because smart people challenge smart people to be smarter. If you want to be lazy, hang outside with the boys that aren't going anywhere. Why? Because you are what you hang around. Our environment tells us a lot about who we think we are, and what we think we deserve. Most of us know someone who has never left the projects, or never tried to do more for themselves. It's not that they are dumb or challenged, it's that they have succumbed to their environment. But the moment you decide to GO HARD, your environment will become a springboard of inspiration to help others to come out of stagnation.

Partners- The people, places and things that we invest the majority of our time into, often become stumbling blocks or diving boards. Diving board relationships are those who see greatness in you, and will help you to spring forth with power and agility. Stumbling blocks are hurdles on a track and field lane. They want you to jump through hoops just to give them attention. And some of them will even make you fall and hurt yourself all because they are in your life to slow you down. The way to "go hard" and to stay purpose-minded, is to remove all stumbling blocks and only attach yourself to diving boards.

Perspective on Experiences: Our experiences are the list of memories, histories, and situations that define our existence. We live because we experience ups and downs. But whether we change or remain the same has a lot to do with how we see our experiences. Most people don't want what they had in their past but they repeat the same behaviors and expect different results. If you are ever going to get to destiny, you're going to have to change your perspective on your experiences. Most people don't understand that everything they have experienced is a set up for something greater to happen.

This is also where Repetitious Information comes in. Why? Because we learn how to live by doing things over and over again. The easiest way to change is to change your pattern. If you want to be in shape, wake up earlier. If you want to fix your marriage, check in more. If you want to start a business, go back to school. A change in pattern changes everything. So without a change, your experiences will limit you. But the moment you change the cycle, your experiences will catapult you into purpose like never before!

So again, I ask you to take some time to smell the roses. Life is moving too quickly for you to live every day in the EXPRESS lane. Answer these questions: don't you want to move on? What are you declaring or speaking over yourself each day? What are you listening to in order to direct you toward destiny? Who are the people that you can name as assets in your life, and who are the liabilities? How are you planning to release them from their duties if they are binding you from becoming everything God intended you to be? Each of these areas is vitally important as you make a decision to GO HARD. The sum total of our life's choices, give us definition and a reputation. As you build your understanding of purpose and destiny, make a decision to change your definition of yourself.

Chapter 4
Matters of the Soul

SOUL RIGHT

If you listen to the popular voices of America, you may be tricked into thinking we are actually a religious nation. You may think that all of us are living a holy and righteous life! After all, we say the pledge of allegiance to the flag, and we declare that we are "one nation, under God." We have "God Bless America" on bumper stickers and campaign ads. People wear Christian paraphernalia all the time—whether it's rosary beads or crosses on our necks or tattoos on our bodies. Even Jesus Christ is a popular symbol in America! Think about the singers or ac- tors who win awards for things that do not glorify God at all, but when they mount the podium to speak, the first thing they say is… "I'd like to give an honor to God… without him, I wouldn't be here to accept this award." Oh yes, we are a go-hard Christian country. We go to church and we shout and praise, and we never really struggle with addiction or jealousy or eviction. Most of what we need from God is said in a short little sermon, and we go home feeling changed, rearranged, and ready to watch the game! Right?
Wrong.

You and I both know that we are frontin'. We are faking it but we are not making it. We talk a good game, but our nation is in debt—Big time! Our families are in trouble, and our churches are barely making it. The numbers of people who say "I'm spiritual but not religious" are growing by the thousands. People are looking for self-help speakers and turning to scientology because the church has not really done its job. And America, well, America has all the nice stuff, but we don't live a life that lines up with the image we portray. We are an image-ridden society, perpetrating truth in the name of "faith," when the reality is, we are further away from God than we've ever been before. We have an outer costume with an inner insanity. And then we wonder why we can't "go hard."

GET TO THE ROOT

Naming this truth caused me to start thinking—what are the root issues of our problems today? Why are we quick to dress up drama on the outside, and quick to cover up pain on the inside? Who is responsible for this clown act we call life? Well, the truth is, all of us are responsible. All of us live into the lie that our greatest value can be seen in what we have materially. We buy things we can't afford, and we borrow things that others think we own, all because we are living a fantasy--and we like it that way!

That's why commercials can convince us to buy anything. Have you ever seen those commercials that are advertising Doritos, but the scene has nothing to do with the chips themselves? What about the car commercials that sell us an ugly car by using a beautiful person to disguise it, (not to mention, most commercials cover up the ridiculous price point, too). Consumerism is plaguing America, and individualism is destroying families, but it's also ruining our perspective. Did you ever think, for once, that perhaps your greatest asset wasn't in the bank? Have you ever stopped to realize that your looks are only surface level strengths, and in a few years, even those won't be able to keep you current? Have you ever thought about the possibility that your greatest power was in something "spiritual;" something that can only be seen after you take full inventory of your soul?

Perhaps you haven't thought about it, but the soul is the focus of this chapter. I want to uncover the lies that we've told ourselves and concentrate on the things that matter most—things like, your will, your emotions, your intellect, your mind, and your imagination. Going hard is a "soul" issue, not just a success issue. You can become successful in life and still have a hole in your soul, all because you didn't take the time to figure out who you really are.

WHO ARE YOU ANYWAY?

Answer that question for me. Who are you? What makes you tick? What gives you the passion to get up in the morning and live? Why do you exist? Beyond your purpose and destiny, what are the core parts of your heart that make your existence important? Who are you without the roles you play, or the kids you raise, or the spouse you cook for? Who are you without the car you drive or the street you live on, or the special parking space you have?

Who are you when nobody sees you? Who are you at night when the lights go out? Paul says, in Romans 7:18-20 some profound words. Consider these verses as you do a quick check of your spirit and soul.

> **For I know that good itself does not dwell in me, that is, in my sinful nature. For I have the desire to do what is good, but I cannot carry it out. For I do not do the good I want to do, but the evil I do not want to do—this I keep on doing. Now if I do what I do not want to do, it is no longer I who do it, but it is sin living in me that does it. Romans 7:18-20**

Paul begins to attack the "who are you?" question by pointing to the war in all of us. Every human being battles with what we want to do versus what we end up doing. I'm sure you wanted to get to work on time, but every day, that old driver got in your way. Now you're unemployed because the boss couldn't take it anymore—but instead of admitting "I am not a punctual person," you blame it on the boss, the old driver, and your wife for getting the kids up later than expected.

Yes, I know you didn't want to get angry and take matters into your own hands, but that nagging, country relative kept yelling at you. She raised her voice, and all of your Bible Study scriptures disappeared. You wanted to do good, but by the end of the night, you were under arrest and she was in the hospital recovering. I guess we won't have a family reunion next year!

Yes, I know you didn't want to cheat on your

spouse, but it's really her fault. You're a man, and you have needs, and she hasn't been paying attention to you! You've been telling her that you have needs, and she's been ignoring you like an alarm clock. So, when the opportunity presented itself, you stayed a few more hours at the job, and you knew the secretary might be there, too. One thing led to another, and now you are in divorce court, trying to figure out child support payments. Why? Because the good that we want to do, does not always translate into what we end up doing.

Paul points to this war as a problem with our soul. All of us are human bodies, but we have a spirit and a soul. The sinful nature knows that we are warring to remain righteousness, and when we let our guard down, it immediately attacks us where it hurts the most. Sin is the very thing that separates us from God. Its power and influence date back to Adam and Eve, where sin entered the world, and life exited humanity. Now, we pray, we read the Word, we go to church, we sing "Hallelujah" and we glorify God in all that we do, but in a blink of an eye, our soul issue rises up. Our soul pulls us off center and depletes our energy. Aren't you tired of starting over? Aren't you tired of regret weighing you down? If so, then you must make a decision to take charge of your soul, and then you will be able to steer straight into destiny!

WHAT IS THE SOUL?

The next obvious question is, "what is the soul?" How do we recognize it? When does it show up? There are many ways to answer this question, but for starters, let me say: the soul is made up of your mind, intellect, emotions, imagination and will. Our soul is the very part of us that makes us human. I once heard a philosopher say, "we have a body, we have a spirit, but we are a soul." The very core part of us that animates the life we live, is the soul. So, the key to going hard in your life and reaching into your next dimension is when you take authority over your mind, your intellect, your emotions, your imagination and your will. We begin that process by letting go of regret, by acknowledging shame, by rebuking fear, by dismissing doubt, by disentangling ourselves from emotional strongholds, and by dispelling insecurities. David said, "bless the Lord oh my soul, and all that is within me." By doing so, he commanded his soul to bless God. He told his soul who the boss of his life was. He commanded his soul not to have control. You can do that too by commanding your soul to line up to the destiny God has for you. Until you take control over your soul, you will never have control over your life.

BUT HOW DO I TAKE CONTROL?

We take control not just by directing and instructing our soul. But we also must examine our patterns and learn to avoid common traps. We all know what traps are? They are places that keep us locked in and bolted down. Familiar traps are those easy tricks that get us to give in every time. Certain people are familiar traps in our lives because when they speak, we start second guessing ourselves. Certain places are familiar traps because the moment we enter that space, we resurrect that which we wish had died. That's why it is so important that a recovering addict remove himself from the environment of influence. If he stays where his ad- diction live, he will never die. He will never be free.

This is exactly how you begin to take control your soul. Avoid traps and walk away. And while you're doing that, replace the void of the world with the voice of the Lord. David said, "thy word have I hid in my heart that I might not sin against thee." In other words, the more Word you hide in your heart, the less space it allows for you to sin. When distractions try to come in, there will be no vacancy for your heart to be filled because you have stocked your heart with the Word. Trust me, an empty heart leaves too much room for you to fall by the trap of a familiar past. When you are serious about going hard, you've got to fill every abscess and close every door.

That means, you don't stay late in the office without a relative coming with you. That means, you call your spouse to check in and let her know when you are on your way home. That means, you count to 10 and take a deep breath before responding to that argumentative relative. That means, you walk away from the mall without buying everything you see. That means, you do not indulge in foods that will cause your blood pressure to rise. That means, you don't lie on your taxes, but you trust God to give you the increase you need because you are a person of integrity and truth.

As you make these different decisions to avoid the trap, think about stocking your heart with the Word of God. Once you allow the word into your heart, it will affect your emotions, and your emotions will affect your actions. Then, your actions will guide you toward positive habits and your habits will become your character. How is destiny guaranteed with this process? Because your character automatically leads you towards the door destiny. Do you see how one building block depends upon another? Do you see how your ability to say "no" today can change your entire future tomorrow? I sure hope you see it. Now...lets go deeper.

5 AREAS OF THE SOUL

If our soul was a house, there are 5 main areas in a house that every person needs: a bathroom, living room, bedroom, kitchen, and storage space. Think about this analogy as I break down the areas of the soul because some of you reading have the wrong stuff in your house. You got couches in your bathroom, and pots in your bedroom! As I said earlier, everything begins in your mind. Philippians 2:5 encourages us to let this mind be in us which was also in Christ Jesus. The more our mind is transformed by Christ, the less damaging our humanness will be.

MIND, EMOTIONS & INTELLECT

The mind is like the kitchen—whatever is in the kitchen will satisfy every part of the house. And if the food is burned in the kitchen, then the entire house will be affected. In the same way, if your mind is burned with negative thoughts and destructive patterns, then your soul is on its way to purgatory!

We also have our intellect—which is something like the bathroom. Why? Because there are moments when you must remember that you have to step away from the crowd, freshen up and present yourself back into the space with clarity, cleanliness, and a new outfit or perspective on life. When our thoughts are in order, then it teaches our brain to step away for a moment and be restored. Our intelligence must grow, over time, and in order to do so, you can't be afraid to be alone. You can't be afraid to read a book or two. Sometimes our soul is suffering because we live in a house with thousands of voices, and we even invite them into our private space of replenishment. As you speak the Word of God over your life, also take the time to step away from it all and refresh your mind. Jesus went to sleep on a boat while others were panicking about a storm. He showed us through his actions how to take control over our soul. If you don't take time for you, then nobody else will!

Our mind is the kitchen, and the intellect is the bathroom. Our emotions tend to be the thing that everyone sees. For that reason, it is the living room. Depending on the furniture in the living room, people will feel welcome or unwelcome. People can see if you are rich or poor. Your living room can't be dying if you call yourself a "go hard" Christian. The way we keep it from dying is by putting our emotions in check. It isn't wise to give your emotions free reign to flip out when they want to, to cry uncontrollably at the White House, and to curse the preacher out in the pulpit. Take control over your soul by filling your heart with the Word, and by decorating your living room with the flowers of life. Speak life over your finances. Speak life over your family. Speak life over your future. And decorate each corner with flowers and mirrors. Each time you enter into your living room, you should see a place that welcomes people into your true heart. Your intellect has been inspired because you take time to read and to learn. Your living room has been decorated so that people can see who you are, and your mind is the kitchen that keeps every part of your house filled with the aroma of fresh bread in the oven. When your mind is fresh, so too is everything else!

IMAGINATION & WILL

Last but not least, we have the imagination and the will. The imagination is the bedroom in our house. It is the place where we dream and rest. It is the place where we can be whoever we want to be. But notice, everyone isn't welcome into your bedroom, so in the same way, you shouldn't expose everyone to your imagination.
Let me tell you about the moment I took control over my imagination. I was always a dreamer but I would have horrible dreams. My dreams would be dark and haunting and I didn't know what was happening to me. But one day, when I confessed this pattern to a friend, he suggested that I take a moment and change the dream. I didn't know what he meant, but he went on to explain that all humans have the power to write their own ending in their dreams. In a man's dreams, he can be anyone and he can do anything. At that moment, I started thinking differently. I started going to sleep with my mind light on.

The next time I had a horrible dream, I decided to change the game. I imagined I had super powers. (stop laughing). I decided to be superman or aqua man, and if I was trapped under water or falling from a building, I was able to tell my dreams that I can make it. My imagination, you see, controlled my victory. And if I could dream it, then certainly, I could be it! I hope you see the big picture of this revelation. Your thoughts—not your mom's influence or your teacher's words—but your thoughts are secret treasures that God governs and protects. When you let down your guard and invite everyone in, it's like someone walking into the studio while you are recording a song; or it's like someone knocking on the door during a standardized test—everyone does not and should not have access to your imagination. Our mind, on a subconscious level, can think about many things. It is an ocean of possibilities that must be guarded by a closed door and a bolted lock. When you give people permission to the tender places of your soul, don't be surprised when they haunt you in your dreams!

Finally, the will of a man is the storage space in your home. Notice, most houses costs thousands of dollars more if the storage capacity is extended. If your house has a basement—a place where most people don't see but a place where the owner can have laundry, miscellaneous items, and an office—then that will make more people attracted to it. Your will is the greatest value of your soul. You know the saying "where there's a will, there is a way." That simply means that if you truly believe it, then you can achieve it. I know it sounds corny, but that slogan is true. Sometimes your will is in the way of your greatest days of success. Think about the show "Biggest Loser." If you see those contestants working hard every day to lose weight, you know it's not because they have physical strength to do so. There is something beyond our physical nature that pushes us to do what we feel we can't do. There's something about the power of your will that will cause a mother to pick up a car with her bare hands if her child is underneath it. Our will can be our strongest asset and also our greatest liability. This is why it belongs in the storage closet.

The storage space is a place where the most important parts of your make-up are put on the shelf. The storage place should be hidden from the general public. Our will is the "human wants" that are the GPS of our existence. When we become Christian, we must stock our wants away and begin each day with the prayer "thy will be done." Our will and our wants may not always be in line with God's will or God's wants for us. Many times, we want something that is rooted in passion, whereas, God wants us to embrace purpose. We want something for the now. God gives us what we need for the eternal. All that we are is locked in our will. How do we get control over our soul? We vow to give our will to God and exchange our wants for his perfect will. Once we surrender our wants to God, then every other part of our spiritual house will fall in line. We, then, are able to allow our intellect to affect our thoughts, and those thoughts will be infiltrated down to our emotions and imaginations. And all of a sudden, what we do in private will mirror who we are in public.

JUST DO IT

I know all of this may seem like a foreign language, but it's simpler than you realize. You have more control over your tomorrow than you have given yourself credit. The only reason you are still broke is because you haven't told yourself anything different. The only reason you are still sad is because you won't allow yourself to paint another picture. The only reason you are carrying other people's drama is because you are too nice and too polite—but it's time you take control of your soul and put people in their place!

The NIKE commercial said it best: JUST DO IT. Sometimes you've got to command your soul to line up. Sometimes you've got to make a decision and choose to change. You have to take control over your anger issues, or you will never be able to keep a relationship. You've got to decide not to bring your credit card to the mall, or else you will never get out of debt. Some things are easier than you realize, but you aren't taking control of your soul!

Your circumstances, experiences, relationships, and even your environment is a direct reflection of the condition of your soul. When your soul is in order, you will be shocked how you will impact the rest of your life.

Chapter 5
You Are NOT the OWNER!

Let me remind you: this book is not intended to be another self- help book that makes you forget about your problems, and commit to something you can't maintain. No, this is a Spirit filled guide that will help you to move past hurt, pain, brokenness, and financial distress once-and-for-all. The first area is relationship with God. And thus far, we have discussed purpose, destiny, the will of God, and the relevance of the soul of man. But having considered all of that, I now want to turn your direction to this reality: you are not your own Creator. You didn't think yourself into the world. No! You have an owner. You have a supervisor. You have a potter. And once we understand our relationship to the potter, and the role that God wants to play in our lives, it will help us to have our GO HARD perspective in order.

> *Yet you, LORD, are our Father. We are the clay, you are the potter; we are all the work of your hand. Do not be angry beyond measure, LORD; do not remember our sins forever. Oh, look on us, we pray, for we are all your people.*
> *Isaiah 64:8-9*

The concept and image that I want you to keep in mind is the image of God as Potter, and humanity as clay. All of us are the clay—no matter how much money we have or don't have, no matter how important we feel or don't feel—we are all clay in the eyes of God. If we see ourselves as clay, we can easily humble ourselves and ascribe greatness to God. Why? because we realize that God is not us. We are not God. The difference between God and us is that we originate from the dust of the earth. God doesn't revolve around our schedule. We exist because we are a part of His! The earth belongs to Him; making us a part of God's plan and not the other way around.

The work of a potter, then, is to mold and form vessels out of clay for the purposes he chooses. These purposes can be for ecclesial reasons, political reasons, practical reasons, for aesthetic pleasure, or for any other reason he deems appropriate, but the most important thing to know is that all things work under the power and providence of God (see Deuteronomy 32:6). We are the workmanship of God's hands. So, like the Israelites, we beg God not to destroy us. We know that no potter will voluntarily destroy his own work. Thus, as clay, we are afforded the opportunity for mercy and favor seeing that God is not unrighteous to destroy the masterfulness of his own creation.

Chapter 6
The Breaking Process

When I decided to allow God to move in my life by way of the Holy Spirit, and I repented so that God could correct the mess in my life, I was able to accept my own mistakes, acknowledge my sin before God, and God didn't have to break me down time and time again. But most of us don't do that automatically. God takes us through trial after trial to humble us and to remold us, to break us and to remake us; all because we are too big-headed to say, "Lord I messed up. Lord I don't know what I'm doing. Lord, HELP ME!"
It is there in the place of stagnancy and stubbornness— the place where we refuse to allow God to work on our mind and we refuse to repent wholeheartedly, that we welcome by omission, the breaking process into our lives.

> *But now, O Lord, You are our Father; we are the clay, and You are our potter; we are all the work of Your hand. Isaiah 64:8*

> *Then the Lord's message came to me. He said, "People of Israel, I can do with you just as this potter does," announces the Lord. "The clay is in the potter's hand. And you are in my hand, people of Israel. Jeremiah 18:5-7*

What if I told you that your inability to embrace God has become your primary disability toward destiny?

In other words, you are the reason you aren't further along. Readers, if you grab onto this revelation, I know it will bless you. In the above verses, we have a visual picture and a dramatic interpretation of the way God sees us. After I truly understood this metaphor in Scripture, it finally clicked for me why God molds us, how God transforms us, and also, why God chooses to do some of the things He does with us during this molding process, as this process can be quite painful and unpleasant at times.

Each part of the process has a different purpose, but consider each step, and think about which area you need to "GO HARDER" in.

Chapter 7
The Water Process

In order to make clay usable and soft enough to mold, the potter must use enough water to make the clay pliable. What good would it be to try to mold a hard-rocky piece of clay? It's like trying to play with play-doe that has been left outside without a lid. The fulfillment of the play-doe depends on the softness of the materials. Thus, water facilitates this process. What is the scriptural representation for water? Answer: The Word of God. The Word of God is not only a light unto our feet, but it is the refreshing revelation from the divine that helps our soul to be quenched by the Spirit of God. It is in this process of water hitting our rocky clay, that we as believers must stay useable and moldable. We do this by allowing the Word of God, which is the symbol of water in Scripture, to have free course in us. By saying yes to the water process, I am saying yes to the Word of God having full control to mold me as God wills.

1. The Word of God needs to be in YOU Before God Can Make You New

Before the clay can be placed on the wheel to make any kind of pottery, there must be enough water in it in order for it to be pliable enough for use. If you are constantly being exposed to the Word of God through worship service, private meditation, conferences and different Christian authors, you should be fit by now for God's use at any time, on any given day. You shouldn't respond to the same things the way you did in previous years. Your situations don't change, your relationships may change, but what's most important is that YOU change. Something about you must be willing to change or you will never get to destiny.

The word of God will transform you if you allow it to. The Scriptures, when applied, will make you more like Christ. The water of the Word is meant to provide moisture for the Holy Spirit, who then takes your unfit clay, and transforms it into what God has predestined you to be. No water, no change. No word, no pottery.

2. You Must Be Properly "Centered" in Jesus Christ

Life without Jesus is a miserable existence. Any good potter knows that after the moisture is applied, the next thing to do is to center the piece of clay onto the electric wheel. This wheel will then begin to spin so that the potter can use his hands in order to mold and shape the clay as it is spinning on the wheel. If you've ever seen the movie "Ghost" I'm sure you know what I'm talking about. The clay moves on the wheel. The wheel is spinning in one slow, predictable pattern. And the potter is moving the clay around with delicate precision, making sure not to let the clay leave from his hand. However, if the piece of clay is not properly centered in the middle of the wheel, then he will not be able to work with it. He will not be able to make the pottery into that which he originally intended. Why? Be- cause centering the clay is key. It is the primary step to being able to make the pot. If he succeeds in making the clay even though it isn't centered properly, the end result will tear apart before the process is finished.

The bottom line is: you have to enter into God's perfect will before God can begin to guide you and mold you into what he has designed for you. You can't go hard if you are off center. A car that does not have a wheel alignment will always bend to the left or the right. You will think you are OK until you reach a certain speed, and then your car will jolt and shake uncontrollably, as a sign that something is not centered.

Think about this question: what are the areas that need centering in your life? Is your income balanced? Is your family life centered? Do you designate time with God alone every day? What areas have been decentered from your life that need to be re-centered? The way toward completely transformation is in your willingness to be centered.

Your life will never go in its rightful direction until you first make a decision to allow the Lord to center you. No center, no surrender. God cannot fully have permission to guide you toward your divine destiny until you grant him "centering" access. This means you must first come to him, let him shape you and mold you, and then allow him to move you where he needs you to go for His perfect use.

Chapter 8
Sanctification

The technical term we use for this process in the church is called sanctification. To be sanctified is to be made over in a slow, steady, and progressive process. If you've ever seen the show "Extreme Home Makeovers," you will be tricked into thinking that makeovers happen overnight. We see the beginning problem and the finished product, but we don't see how long it took to remodel the home, where the furniture was purchased, the different paint options they had to consider, or the permits they had to buy in order to build in the area they were in. There are many hidden doors in the house of sanctification, most of which, your visitors never see. Why? Because sanctification is a cleansing process that happens between you and God. The key to sanctification is patience. We must have patience with the Lord and with one another, so that God can work and build our lives in his timing, and not ours. In our fast-paced, self-centered world, we are accustomed to instant everything. But in God's realm, He usually works things out at a much slower pace.

If we do not learn how to go with His slower flows and slower time frames, we will become very frustrated and impatient. But let me remind you again: you are not the owner. Your vehicle of life, filled with purpose and destiny, has been purchased by God. He made the way for you in order to drive you into a life of prosperity and peace. You have two options: to go hard or to go home. Going home means that you will take the keys back from God and tell him, "I know what I'm doing." Going hard means you will keep on reading to see how you can move from relationship with God to your relationship with others.

SECTION TWO
RELATIONSHIP WITH YOURSELF

Chapter 9
Seize the Day

There is a phrase rarely used in today's generation, but it has significant meaning. It's a Latin expression: 'Carpe Diem," which means "seize the day." This expression reminds us just how important it is to take advantage of every second, every minute, and every hour of each day. Let's face it: life is a quick rollercoaster. It seems to take forever to take off, but once you reach a certain point, you can't seem to stop it from spiraling. One second you are giving birth to your child. The next second, you are teaching her how to ride a bike without training wheels. And almost immediately, you are taking pictures at her wedding as you hand her off to her lawfully wedded husband. Life is a quick-paced non-stop flight. After you board, it is sure to take you up quick and drop you even quicker. So if you don't take the time to pay attention, your entire life will pass you by and you will pay bills, buy homes, work your way up to the top, and not know how and when you got there.

For this reason, I need to introduce this phrase, "Carpe Diem," because much of our destiny is tied to how often we pay attention. Most of the greatest gifts in life are right in front of us, but we don't see them because we are so busy trying to have width but no depth. I'm sure you know people like that: they would prefer to have 10 colleagues than to have 2 friends. It takes time to deepen friendship, but it also makes you a shallow person if you can't trust the people who are around you on a daily basis. Which do you prefer? How is your life looking these days? Are you rushing to get everywhere or is life slowing down to meet your demands? Can you keep and maintain strong friendships, or do you find yourself recycling people like water bottles on the side of the road? When you make a concerted effort to seize the day, you align your life in direct proportion to God's blessings.

Think for a moment about what you do know about your life and what you don't know. How much more time will you be on earth? How many more beats will your heart pump? What imprint or impact has your life left on the world? Does anyone else know you outside of your family? Your church? Your job? Are you living a life that you would be happy to show others? Are you smiling more than you are crying? Do you regret more situations than you remember? Take some time to have a "carpe diem" moment. It is only when we reflect on the progress of our past that we can make changes toward a better future. Some of you reading are begging for change. Your future is begging for your attention. Your destiny is begging for your commitment. So since you don't know how much you have left, maximize on what you do have: TODAY.

Chapter 10
Pluck the Day

In the literal sense, 'Carpe' literally means 'to pluck', with particular reference to the picking of fruit. So, a more accurate rendition or translation of this phrase is 'enjoy the day, pluck the day when it is ripe'. The extended Latin version is: 'CARPE DIEM, QUAM MINIMUM CREDULA POSTERO' which translates as 'Pluck the day, trusting as little as possible in the future.' Why does this matter? It matters because half of your time is spent wondering about the fear of failing tomorrow, when you've already failed by not doing what should've been done today. Let me say it another way: Today is looking you in the face and asking, "what about me?" Because every moment you wake up, you are planning for the BIG MOMENT that may never happen. You are rehearsing for the big production that can only manifest when and if you perform well at the local theatre. You are excited about becoming a bestselling author, but you haven't finished your first chapter! PLUCK the DAY! Get the fruit out of the garden for today's meal. Because if you don't eat today, you won't be alive to see tomorrow!

Do you get it! I have come to light fire under your motivation. You cannot live in "la la" land and call it "faith." Real faith MOVES even when it sees no evidence. Real faith responds even if the phone doesn't ring. Real courage dreams again, even after it has messed up in times past. The moment we stop our momentum because of one bad mistake, we empower our past to disable our future. PLUCK THE DAY! Move out of the neutral posture of "idealism," and surrender yourself to real issues and questions that are showing up in your life on a daily basis.

When you pluck something, I'm sure you already know that plucking is uncomfortable business. Do you know a mother or elder in the church who still will pluck the children if they misbehave during the sermon? If you do, or if you've been plucked, you know it is a sharp and sometimes painful experience. The reason that plucking causes pain is because something must be broken in order for the fruit to have value to the human body. In other words, I can see the apple growing from the tree, but until I pluck it out, it can serve no true purpose for me. And like that apple dangling on the branch of a tree, many of us are looking at our tomorrow hoping that God will send the wind necessary to cause it to drop down into our laps. We won't go looking for a job because we expect it to fall from the tree. We won't pursue another degree because we expect it to fall from the tree. We're afraid to date again because we were hurt many times before, so we allow our fear to keep us stunted, and instead of trying again, we look up in the sky, asking God why, and waiting for God to do for us what we can do for ourselves.

If I were speaking about this in church, I might say something right now like "look at your neighbor and say, PLUCK IT OUT!" Plucking is painful. Plucking is forceful. Plucking may even cause embarrassment. But plucking is necessary. Let me say it like this: if you knew that destiny was within arm's reach, wouldn't you pluck it? IF you knew that you were only one pluck away from having the greatest life you could ever imagine…would you stretch out and do something you've never done before?

I sure would!

This is why "Go Hard" is your literary coach pushing you to try again. You have two options: to believe your past or to try again. Both options require faith. But which will you choose?

Chapter 11
Living a FULL Life

In the bible, these words are found in Psalm 90:12- - So teach us to number our days, that we may gain a heart of wisdom." This is a reminder that each and every one of us must take a look at our lives and ask the grand question: "Am I Living Life according to God's fullest idea of it?" If you are honest with your answer, you will admit that you are holding back. You are skeptical of success. You are nervous about becoming what you know your potential has prepared you to become. If you are honest, you are holding your breath as you read this chapter. Why? Because something on the inside is telling you, "this is for you" but doubt keeps fighting to keep you numb and neutralized.

The reason we must turn the page from relationship with God to relationship with people, is because people often hold us back from becoming what God has prepared us to be. People, friends, and family members can become strongholds in our lives. They become our greatest obstacles because we go to them for approval and affirmation. And sometimes, no matter how nice a person is, we can't go to a king to ask him how to be a prophet. The two roles don't match! So Jeremiah, you are a prophet to the nations. Why would you go to Josiah, who is a king, to receive advice on how to prophesy? His counseling is only as good as his experience, and what if your experiences are supposed to be different? What if you were created to inspire the very people you are most intimidated by? What if you need to seize the day so that you can hire Josiah in ten years? What if you will one day become the teacher and the people you respect and esteem the most, will become your students? What if the thing that is blocking you from destiny is the person who needs your boldness in order for them to follow suit?

Chapter 12
I am my Worst Enemy!

Family and friends may be obstacles, but in my life, I can't blame them because the truth of the matter is, I have been my worst enemy! I am a person. I am a human being. And because I have a mind, emotions, and feelings, I can sometimes sabotage my own success all because I am expecting to fail. I create a "just in case" file because I don't believe in ME! My greatest threat isn't Satan…it's ME! If my life hit movie theatres, I would be both the beauty and the beast, or the Jekyll and the Hyde. The culprit holding me back from some of the greatest moments in life…has been ME!

So, let's put our cards on the table. Am I alone in this area? Do you, too, find yourself sabotaging your success? If so, what are you weak- nesses? What are the things you do that hold you back from optimal success? I will share one of my weaknesses with you. Quite honestly, I tell everyone that I work well under pressure, (and I do), but behind that strength is a weakness called procrastination. I am a consummate procrastinator, especially when what I want to avoid pain. None of us like pain, but listen, I can't stand it! So, I have trained myself to wait until the very last moment to endure it—whether it's having a painful conversation or enduring a painful workout—my antipathy toward pain causes me to drag my feet as I inch my way toward the races.

Every one of us, if our issue is not procrastination—it is certainly something else! We all have been guilty of knowing the right thing to do and waiting until the last moment to do it. And most times, we wait because we want to avoid the inevitable, but here is the good news: most pain is not meant to kill you. Instead, it is intended to make you stronger.

Chapter 13
The Pain of Loss

Let me break this down to some concrete examples. Think about the pain of losing something—losing a friend, losing respect, or losing ground when you feel like you have come so far. When I first got married, my wife and I went through a painful financial season. It was tough because we found ourselves in between living conditions. We sold our home and couldn't find another home that we could afford. So, we had to make a choice: we could either move in with her father or move in with my parents. At the time, those options seemed emasculating. As a man, I didn't want to lose my dignity or manhood by moving in with my in-laws. But after prayer, I realized that God was teaching me how to get rid of pride. God was teaching me how to be flexible. He was also teaching me that what makes a family is not the house you build, but the home you nurture.

I got a revelation even though it wasn't what I wanted to hear. I learned in that season that I wasn't less of a man if I moved in with my folks, I was less of a man if I refused the help I was being given. So I asked for help. We decided to move in with my mother and father in my old bedroom. It was a cozy place, to say the least, measuring in at 10x15. Go ahead ... do the math. There were three people in one room, and it was tighter than a shoe box, but we had to make it work.

All the dynamics of this situation made life more challenging because I felt like I was losing so much with this move. But I kept my mind on the prize and realized: sometimes you have to take one step backwards in order to move forward. The pain of financial strain, and the pain of procrastination taught me to have work ethic. I never thought I could muster up the strength to pave my own way, but that eventually helped me to run my own business and lead my own family. I made my mind, in that cozy little room, that I would never be in this 10X15 again. I determined to work hard and move my family to another level, and I did. The pain pushed me to a place of determination and to be honest, if I wasn't pressed to do it then, I don't know if I could've manifested it later.

What if the same thing is true for you? What if your most painful moments are lesson plans for your greatest successes? What if your experiences are making you stronger, wiser, better, and more coherent? If you look at your pain as an enemy, you will never grow past your own level of control. But if you see pain as a fitness trainer, you will exercise better because of it. If you envision pain as the life coach guiding you through difficulty, you will allow it to teach you something that life could've never shown you without it! It all boils down to perspective. How you envision your enemy determines how influential that enemy will be in your life.

Chapter 14
The Outcome of Pain

The second kind of pain that typically causes us not to seize the moment is the outcome of pain. You know what it's like to break a bone, I'm sure. Most people who experience a broken arm or a broken joint will tell you that the initial pain is one thing, but the outcome of that pain is another. In other words, you don't feel the pain until your life has to adjust to its ramifications. Now you can't play baseball for two weeks—because your muscles are healing. Now you have to go back out on the work force and find a job. I'm sure that cursing your boss out felt good at the moment, but the outcome of that conversation, caused you irreparable damage. I'm sure the affair felt good while the encounter was happening, but when you realized that your mistake would rip your family apart, and cause tension in the household, you started wishing that you didn't have to endure the pain, if it came with the side effects of a horrible outcome.

What are the painful experiences you've been avoiding, all because you are afraid of the outcome? Many people have a tendency to focus so much on what hasn't happened yet, that they disqualify themselves from making a decision. Yes, some painful situations you can avoid—those things you do that are rooted in selfishness, can and should be avoided. But there are some healthy pains that will grow you and grow others. In order to get the juice out of those experiences, you have got to be squeezed into painful moments. You've got to move beyond thinking about it and just decide to do it! Usually when we are being challenged to grow in one area, we become our greatest enemy. We conclude that if the outcome doesn't happen the way we expect it, we will become distraught and humiliated—so before we even "go hard" for it, we just go home. We decide to stay comfortable. We continue to feed sheep in the field, like David did, because we're good at shepherding, but what if God has a kingdom waiting for you to rule and reign? You won't get there until you step out of your comfort zone.

Here is a word of encouragement for each of you experiencing this kind of pain. The key to breaking the curse of self-sabotage is when you determine to push yourself past your comfort zone and try again. Think about how many women have heard the doctor say "you can't have a baby." And yet, months later, they are pregnant and enjoying fruit from a tree they thought would never harvest anything. Think about how many "one hit wonders" stood outside long audition lines, pressing beyond their comfort zone and now they are on top of the billboard charts and traveling across the world. Why are Christians the last group of people who are willing to come out of the closet and challenge the norm? Everyone else is bold enough to "go hard," and yet we are comfortable staying home and praying in our secret closet.

There is nothing wrong with prayer, but sometimes, you've got to pray with your eyes open. Sometimes, you've got to pray on your way to the interview. Sometimes you've got to see God outside of your gender, race, or nationality.

What if the door you are trying to go through is too small for the God that is leading you? Don't sabotage your own success in the name of spirituality. Instead, take a leap of faith and start walking out on the water! It is very possible to walk and pray at the same time. It is very possible to trust God for the house and apply for the house at the same time. The worst you can hear is "no!" And if you're like me, I'm not afraid of "no." I'm afraid of regret. So, try again. Step out of your comfort zone and heal yourself. Until you get delivered from the box you put your God in, God can never show himself as bigger than the perspective you have of Him. Until you are willing to fire "comfort" in order to hire purpose, you will never reach destiny. Your pain must become ammunition toward success— otherwise, you won't succeed!

Chapter 15
The Process of Pain

The third pain gripping many of us is the most difficult area of them all—it's what I call, the process of pain. Of course, everything in life—whether it is education or work or marriage or love or real estate or buying a car, comes with a process. So, too, does pain. Pain brings a process to your doorstep that can literally cause you to stop in your tracks. Whether it's the pain of foreclosure, or the pain of divorce, when it comes to your life, all normal ways of being are discontinued. The game is paused. The dinner is burned. The tears become rivers. The kitchen talk becomes cold. The people listening become mummies. Hearts become hardened. Neighbors become gossipers. Friends become paranoid. The church becomes silent. Pause. *Why is the church seemingly silent when people are going through the process of pain?*

Why is it easier for most people to hear a sermon about the promise or the prison, but not about the process? It is a most difficult area to deal with, but if you're going to be equipped to handle your greatest enemies, you cannot run from the process. You can't run away from the battle—you've got to be willing to fight. Half of the time, the reason people end up in jail serving a greater sentence than the actual crime committed, is because they tried to avoid the process. The cop flagged them down, and they sped up instead of pulling over. Now, they have more issues on top of the initial reason they got pulled over. The celebrity received a notice from the IRS to pay her taxes. She swept it under the rug, and now five years later, she's being charged with negligence on top of her overdue taxes. What am I trying to say? I'm saying, you can't avoid the process of pain.

In scripture, we see that avoided pain, but in the process, he only made things worse. When David committed adultery with Bathsheba, he thought to himself, "let me fix this by avoiding that." Here's a word to the wise: you can never fix "this" by avoiding "that." So, he invited her husband, Uriah, to leave the battlefield for a few days, hoping that Bathsheba's husband would sleep with his wife and cover up David's sin. But the man was so dedicated to his position that he never went home. David tried to get the man drunk, but nothing he did to cover up the process, worked in the long run.

Eventually, the poor man was killed. David conspired to have him murdered on the front line of war, and what should've ended in confession, resulted in death. The lesson here is simple: endure the process and you will avoid death. Even if you are the enemy in the story, endure the process and your spirit will live. Your family will live. Your finances will bounce back. But you've got to endure the process.

I know that most of us want to be the victim or the victor. We want to be the protagonist and the problem-solver. But what happens when you are the culprit? What do you do when it's your fault? I'll tell you what you do:

you "go hard" and own up to what you did. I'll tell you what you do: tell the truth by any means necessary. I'll tell you what you do: you spend the next season of your life in recovery. Why? Because the process of pain won't last forever. If you delay it or deny it, it will haunt you for a lifetime. But you can't avoid it another day in the name of procrastination. Some things hurt, but no pain lasts forever. Let the process run its course, and it will be over before you know it.

I'm not sure who I am writing to, but I began this chapter confessing my own weaknesses. I told you where I am still struggling not to be my own enemy, but where are you struggling? What are your weaknesses and challenges? Where do you need to be better? Don't blame dad or mom. Don't blame your wife and kids. Look at yourself and be honest. What is it that you continue to do that stunts your own growth? What painful processes are you avoiding? What painful habits are you employing? Are you disorganized? Are you struggling with an addiction? Do you have trouble maintaining a budget? Are you an over-spender, or an over-eater? Do you tend to blame others for what you need to take responsibility for? Answering these questions will put you on the road to recovery. It will also allow you to get past the season of pain so that you can move on to the season of promise!

SECTION THREE
RELATIONSHIP WITH PEOPLE

The previous sections have been about God, about purpose and destiny, and about YOU. Along the way, we have learned the difference between our body, our spirit, and our soul. We have learned that we are not the Potter, but we are simply the clay. We are not the driver, we are the passengers. We have also learned how to become better masters of our destiny by yielding to the process of pain. Like any other human being in the world, nobody likes pain. But if we overcome the painful experiences, we can become the best person that God intended us to be.

Of the most painful encounters in life, there is no worse pain than to be hurt by someone you love. Our deepest let downs are the result of significant investment into people's live. If we were self-absorbed and narcissistic, we could get stabbed in the back by a loved one, remove the knife, and keep it moving. And after a few days, the scar would heal, the blood would cease, and we would be right back on our feet, doing what we were called to do. But there is something about a relationship that can stagnant your growth. Relationships can also catapult you into the future. There's something about a positive role model that can put you on the right path, or a negative one that can steer you away from purpose.

This section will discuss our relationships with people—most specifically our loved ones. I want to make a distinction between what we put our faith in, and what we invest our fears in. Everything, you will come to learn after reading this chapter, grows from the seed of faith or the seed of fear. Most of that fear, for human beings, derives from our definition of whole-ness. Let me explain what I mean by that. Have you ever met a girl who felt like she was incomplete until she figured out who her husband was? Or maybe you know a guy that is promiscuous because he cannot find fulfillment in his own bed alone. Instead, he needs to work his proverbial "black book" until he has enjoyed company with almost every girl in his state. Why? Because he fears being alone. He is not whole. He is broken and in need of repair. Therefore, his understanding of life is wrapped up in giving his body to someone else. And in part, both of these examples are on to something.

The Bible tells us that we were not created to be alone. In fact, when God saw that Adam was alone, He created Eve so that Adam could have company, and enjoy life with someone. So, yes, it is right for us to long for relationship; but no relationship should become your god. You should never feel like you are nothing without the company of other people. If you set yourself up to believe that you are insignificant without others, then you will also allow yourself to be defined by and confined by others. That means - if they don't want to eat, you won't eat. If they don't want to go to church, you won't want to go to church. If they are not ready to change, you won't be ready to change. Do you know people like this? They wait for someone else to dictate the destiny of their lives, all because they do not understand how to relate to people. They don't have a good sense of boundaries and control. They have lost their own voice trying to audition for others' approval. And unless your guiding light is God, you will always fail human beings. You will never measure up to their expectations, because you weren't made to please them. You were made to please God.

So, yes, you are absolutely right---we were not created to be alone, but we were also not designed to be desperate. You are too wonderful to be desperate. You are too creative and unique to be any- body's contingency clause. God has a community waiting for you to be a part of, but before He reveals who those people are, or who that spouse is, He wants you to conquer your fear by becoming whole all by yourself.

Chapter 16
Real Fulfillment

Listen to the words of Tom Robbins. I think what he says in a few lines, is an eye-opener for people who want to GO HARD in their interpersonal relationships. He writes: "When we're incomplete, we're always searching for somebody to complete us. When, after a few years or a few months of a relationship, we find that we're still unfulfilled, we blame our partners and take up with somebody more promising. This can go on and on--series polygamy--until we admit that while a partner can add sweet dimensions to our lives, we, each of us, are responsible for our own fulfillment. Nobody else can provide it for us, and to believe otherwise is to delude ourselves dangerously and to program for eventual failure every relationship we enter."

This quote speaks to all kinds of relationships. Whether you are in a romantic relationship, a business relationship, a church relationship, a familial, platonic relationship, or an internal relationship, the point still remains—your completeness must be found in Christ and not in the cushion of other people around you. If the person you love the most leaves you tomorrow, what will you do? Will you hide under a bed and cry your life away? Will you forsake every goal and shut down every dream? I hope you won't. If you are really ready to dive toward destiny, you've got to conquer your fear of flying, and prepare for the possibility that you will have to go after it alone. Aloneness isn't a disease, it is your vitamin C. It gives you the strength to make it without depending on others. It gives you the confidence necessary to trust God without the props of people's wavering opinions. Great warriors win because they see the team as optional, and not as a requirement. If your mom doesn't come to the game, you can still win the tournament. If daddy doesn't show up to your recital, that doesn't mean you are a poor dancer. That means that he is missing out on one of life's greatest moments. But the issue isn't you—it's him!

Real winners must have enough courage to fight Goliath without Saul's armor; without a band of cheerleaders. If they show up, wonderful! But if they don't, it doesn't matter! Why? Because you are so focused on being the best YOU that you can be, you don't even see their presence or absence until you have won.

Nobody is responsible for filling your purpose tank but God. Proverbs 3:5 tells us where to deposit our trust dollars. It reads "trust in the Lord with all your heart and lean not unto your own understanding. In all thy ways, acknowledge him, and he shall direct your path." I want to help you to build better relationships with people, but in order to do so, you've got to have a solid relationship with yourself. How can you love your wife as you love yourself, if you don't love yourself? How can you respect a stranger, if you treat yourself like a stranger? Our trust dollars must be de- posited in the bank of heaven. Only God deserves ownership of your most valuable treasures. Only God deserves the secret password to your vulnerability. If you can learn how to put more stock in your God account, and not in your "human approval" account, then you would be a better human being. Don't lean unto your own understanding. People change just as quickly as the stock market. But if you learn to ask God for proper understanding, then you will never fall victim to co-dependency.

Chapter 17
Encourage Yourself

Learn to be the master of your own fulfillment or you will never be fulfilled. You cannot wait for others to wake up, you have to wake up and make your own coffee, or you will never smell the coffee. Stop waiting on people to validate you; validate yourself! Stop waiting on a supervisor to encourage you; encourage yourself!
In 1 Samuel 30, David experienced great loss. After going out to fight a significant battle, he comes home to discover that all of his family members and friends have been taken from him. Have you ever had your very life flipped upside down? Do you remember what it was like to realize that your life would never be the same again? I'm sure in that moment, David wanted to give up on relationships. I'm sure he wanted to throw in the towel and take his very life. But the Scripture gives us the key to maintaining a GO HARD mentality. That key is self-encouragement. To encourage oneself means to look in the mirror and state who you are. Self-encouragement sees beyond the present calamity of today, and focuses on the promises of God. It is the human being becoming a spiritual being. It is focusing on the future, and not becoming hypnotized by the now.

David didn't wait for a prophet to tell him who he was. He didn't wait to land a key interview with Oprah Winfrey. David realized something that we still struggle to understand. Donald Lawrence wrote it, and many churches have sung it, but the fact remains: sometimes you've got to encourage yourself. The key to moving forward is when you have the tenacity to look in the mirror and tell yourself what you wish others would tell you. Take away their power by claiming victory over yourself. You are not broke. Life is not over. You are intelligent. You are capable. You can make it. You will achieve. You can do all things through Christ which strengthens you. This mountain will be moved in Jesus' name. God is able to do exceedingly, abundantly, above all that you can ask or think. You are the head and not the tail. You are above and not beneath. You are the lender and not the borrower. You are the first and not the last.

These words of affirmation will help you get out of the bed on days when you don't want to live. I know you've been at a low place, but take authority over your mind, and speak life to your situation. Encourage yourself by backing up from the cliff of "throwing it all away." You will not die, but you will live says the Lord. Every situation is for your making, not for your breaking. Think about how far you've come to get here. If you let go now, you will never change the cycle in your family. Think about how God has been with you in situations far more difficult in times past. So if God did it before, then He is faithful to do it again!

When you encourage yourself, you awaken the soul into praise. When you encourage yourself, you attract encouragers. Sometimes, the right kind of self-encouragement will welcome the right kind of people into your life. What if your help is waiting on you to make the first step? After David encouraged himself, a messenger from the opposing army helped him to discover and recapture his family. What if God is placing people in your life to recover all, but he's waiting on you to make the first step? Come on, do it. Don't delay another day. Just encourage yourself. Your courage is waiting behind the door of self-encouragement. Do you know who you are? You have been independently contracted by God to do His work in the earth. Understand what I'm saying—you are important to God, and no man lives on an island. So yes, we all need one another to survive. But at the same time, you CAN make it without the life support of other people around you. If your family decides to drop you, God is still with you. If your friends disappear, you are more than the sum total of your friendships. If the church misunderstands you, there are other churches willing to accept you with open arms. Many times, it's just a shift in perspective. If you would just believe that you are capable of GOING HARD without the fans and crowd-pleasers, then you will go farther than you could ever imagine! Simply believe that God has greater for you, and you will welcome new relationships into your life that will sow into your future and not suck the very life out of you.

Chapter 18
Fear Factor

Have you ever heard the nursery stories about the girl who was afraid of the monster under her bed? She would run to mommy and ask her to look under the bed, and then minutes after her mother left the room, she would see the shadow of what appeared to be a monster, looming out at her once again. When the mother finally turned on the light, the little girl realized that she was only afraid of a shadow—it was a figment of her imagination. Something from the closet appeared to be a monster, but it was, in all actuality, light projected in the wrong place. What if the same situation is happening to you? What if God is trying to bring you new friends and new relationships, but because of the shadow of let downs experienced last year, you are afraid to open up again?

The same way the little girl was afraid of the dark, David was afraid of walking through the valley. But here is the revelation. The valley wasn't the problem. It was the shadow of death that was in the valley! Here is the verse in Psalm 23:

> **The Lord is my shepherd; I shall not want. He maketh me to lie down in green pastures: he leadeth me beside the still waters. He restoreth my soul: he leadeth me in the paths of righteousness for his name's sake. Yea, though I walk through the valley of the shadow**

of death, I will fear no evil: for thou art with me; thy rod and thy staff they comfort me. Thou preparest a table before me in the presence of mine enemies: thou anointest my head with oil; my cup runneth over Surely goodness and mercy shall follow me all the days of my life: and I will dwell in the house of the Lord forever.

Wait, did you catch that! I know this is a very familiar passage but I want you to read it again as if you have never read it before. With fresh eyes, you will realize something spectacular! It wasn't even death that was haunting David. What appeared to be death to David, was only a shadow in reality. It was "bad lighting," which planted a negative thought into his mind that wasn't there all along. Some of us have moved across the country because of "bad lighting." Some of us have quit our jobs be- cause of bad lighting. Some of us have left the church because of bad lighting. Bad lighting is the "appearance of evil" and the bark of a dog that doesn't have a bite. Bad lighting is when you look once and think it's a ghost, but when you look twice, you realize it's just fog in the dawning of the day. What I am saying is simple, but it will change your life if you grasp it fully. When you truly see that what you feared the most was just a shadow, you will realize and know for sure that the monster under your bed, was only in your mind—and it wasn't a real monster after all!

The way David conquers his fear is by realizing, "thou are with me." In other words, David was not in this valley alone. God was with Him. God was the security guard who guided him to safety. God's presence was like twelve body builders next to Him. God, the maker of the universe, was holding David's hand in the midst of a dark night and a troubled time. One of the greatest moments in life is when you realize that God is with you. I know you are upset that he forgot about you, or that she didn't call you back, but God is with you! And that is why you have no reason to fear. You give life to fear every time you forget that God is there. Every time you pretend that God is the shadow, and that death is the reality, you give life to a dead thing. But the key to deliverance is when you decide to flip the script. All of us must flip the script of fear and turn on the light of faith if we're going to conquer "the shadow of death." Whatever appears to be dying in your life—your motivation, your skill, your career, your zeal, your joy, your family, your finances—you've got to determine in your mind to see the truth behind the lie. Most of what you see is fiction or a fairy tale. It's just a shadow. It is not evil; it is the "appearance of evil." With a little light adjustment, the thing you once feared will later become a light affliction you've conquered. The bench press that was once weighing you down will end up being a 20-pound dumbbell used for "warm-ups" in the gym. Your new fitness of faith begins with a shift in perspective.

Chapter 19
The Bigger Picture

I know you are going through something major right now, so I don't want to downplay your situation. I just want to give you, or rather show you, the big picture. Each of us can identify with being afraid of something or someone. We all know what it's like to be emotionally attacked by fear. My personal experiences are just two or three episodes of fear that almost made me throw in the towel. But once I learned the purpose of the "shadow," I was able to push past those fears, and embrace the next level God had designed for me.

It was a hot summer day, and I could barely drink enough water to stay cool. I was serving as a youth pastor at the time, and as such, I was responsible for completing many pastoral duties like hospital visits, summer programs for kids and various other administrative tasks. All of the work began to affect my stamina, and all of a sudden, I felt weak in my body. Have you ever felt that kind of weakness where you just knew, in moments, you were about to faint? That was me, that day, in that scorching summer heat. In my weakness, I paused to ask God for strength. I needed to finish my work, but I felt like I was going to faint any minute.

In that short prayer, I heard God speaking the word "more." I couldn't believe my ears, so I quieted my spirit again. I thought perhaps God had meant to send that message to someone else. But no. Once again, I heard the word "More." God wanted me to do more, and I was already drained and feeling maxed out. It seemed like the more I served, the more God wanted me to serve. It was like an unending to do list. The moment I crossed off 5 tasks for the day, 15 more found their way on the list!

I brushed it off and tried to get back into my day. But, God wasn't done with the "MORE" message. Shortly after this, I found myself driving down to the shore with my wife and two children. I heard the Lord say, "I'm about to move you, so get ready." On top of all that I was doing, now God wanted to move me? Are you serious, Lord? I was happy with my salary, benefits, and the other amenities of ministry. I didn't really want to move on top of all of this, but then again, God was pushing me for more. While He was trying to strengthen my faith, I found myself giving into fear. I wasn't a single man anymore. I was now in relationship with three other people— my wife and two kids—and I needed the Lord to slow down a little bit and help me make a wise choice for my family.

Let me pause and talk to those who feel responsible for the family God has entrusted them with. It is scary to trust God for yourself, but it is even more difficult to trust God for others whom you feel responsible for. What got me through this moment was when I realized that these members of my family—were also covered by God's protection. In fact, I was only the steward over my loved ones. God owned them and allowed me to lease them for a limited time. That calmed me down because I realized that God was in control of all of us. I wasn't the one coordinating our steps. God was ordering each and every one of our moves, and He trusted me to watch over my family. I wasn't the decider or the employer—I was just the gardener entrusted to tend to the Master's garden until he returned. Learning this helped me to gain better insight about my relationships with people.

If we remember that we do not own anyone, but God has leased them to us for a limited time, it will help us to handle them differently. People are fallible and unpredictable. They can say or do the wrong thing, but if you remember that they belong to God, then like the babysitter who won't reprimand someone else's children, you will not abuse those who do not belong to you. Like the protective parent that He is, God is watching every move you make. Every response you give is under His surveillance, so if you're going to fear anything, fear Him—not them! Only fear what God will do if you mishandle his people, because it is his job to make sure you all are taken care of. This is not just for nuclear families, this is for pastors, for teachers, for professionals, and for surrogate parents all around the world!

But let me continue the story, because these episodes will, I hope, deliver you from the stronghold of fear. As I was taking a trip down to the shore, the Lord began to speak. I knew He was trying to increase my faith, but I was settled on fear. I was comfortable. I didn't know what "more" meant, and I didn't think I had a good handle over what He had already given me. But God truly knows what you can handle. You may think you have reached your max, but the moment you think you can't do anything else, He will drop another responsibility in your lap! Why? Because He re- ally knows you better than you know yourself. So, there we were---afraid to say "no" to God, but hesitant to say yes. My wife had the same uncomfortable feeling, but we didn't know what to do with it all.

Chapter 20
F.E.A.R Defined

I was fearful of the next step for my life, for my family and for my financial situation. Questions were racing in my head— where will we go, where will we live, how will we make it, will we be poor? I knew what the Word said. I had quoted it all the time that "God would supply my needs according to His riches in glory" but it's very easy to quote a scripture mindlessly until you need that scripture to come alive. That was when I realized: I had given my life over to fear. I was looking at all of the evidence, and I wasn't trusting the voice of the Lord. The definition of fear became strikingly apparent in that moment. FEAR is nothing but **False Evidence Appearing Real!** I had no reason to feel this way, but fear was gripping me and affecting my interactions with my wife and kids.

What if fear is the culprit keeping you stagnant? What if it's not about your income, or you're your excuses? I know you dropped out of school, and I know you don't have the best record, but what if your real struggle is between the voices in your head telling you that you will never make it because of every excuse that you have accepted as truth? That is what fear comes to do—to turn your faith upside down, and it does so by presenting false evidence that isn't even real. The lump on your breast was a mosquito bite. But now you're walking around telling everyone that you have stage 4 cancer. The pink slip from the boss was just a note telling you that your wife called you. But the moment you saw it, you started applying for other jobs. The evidence from the enemy always appears to be the thing that will shake you up but learn to see it for what it is. Deception is only a shadow. Nothing under that bed is going to destroy you, because the enemy can do nothing to us unless God allows it. There is a Master Architect orchestrating every move in your life. If God hasn't told you to worry about it, then fear is trying to steer you off course.

I had a choice to make that day—to believe the report of the Lord, or to sign my life away to the threats of the enemy. I made a decision to be faithful, to be fruitful and to be focused. I became more faithful on my job, and woke up to the reality that the enemy wanted me to forfeit my current place prematurely. The work that once seemed overwhelming, was now easy and I breezed through it. I became more fruitful in conversation with my wife. We grew as a couple because we realized that a family was not defined by the size of their house, but by the size of their love. I became focused on what God was saying to me that day. Many of us worry about tomorrow and fail to do what God told us to accomplish today. My focus became a 24-hour window of time. If it didn't need to be done today, I would reserve my energy toward it, for tomorrow. There was too much to be done for me to drain myself over things I couldn't change. I suspect the same is true for you. God has put too much in you today for you to worry about tomorrow. FEAR is only false evidence appearing real. Its mission is to keep you from destiny by causing you to forfeit every God-ordained relationship.

But God will strengthen you to embrace those around you who are purpose-filled, and helpers to your vision. You can't do this alone, so choose to be faithful, be fruitful and be focused. And once you do that, you will become a master of your relationships with people.

Chapter 21
What's Love Got to Do with It?

There is no way we can talk about relationships without talking about love. Love is one of the most overused verbs in the dictionary. To some, it is a just a human emotion. To others, it is a tingly feeling that shows up when you meet someone you like. Still, another might define love as suffering—Jesus, for example, died on the cross because of love. In fact, scripture tells us that the greatest love act that ever happened was from this man named Jesus who laid down his life for his friends—which in actuality, were enemies at the time. So love can be defined in many ways.

Some people have a very unhealthy definition of love. To them, if their spouse hits them at night, that is love. Or if their boss cheats them out of their check, he or she is doing it out of love. But love isn't abusive. Love isn't controlling or manipulative. Love is what love does. Love doesn't search for a discount. Godly love goes HARD after what it desires. It is an investment in the future even when the present seems difficult. Love is the power and discipline to endure until the end despite the temptation to throw in the towel. Love is seen when that married couple of 60 years holds one another as the husband kisses his wife goodbye for the last time. Love is felt when a newborn enters the world, and the mother grabs her child for the first time. Love is in the details. Love is seen in the space between what people read about you. Love is in the obvious, and love is in the subliminal. Love is the reason you wake up every day to feed a household full of children who never say, "thank you." It's love that inspires you to pray when you feel like crying, or worship when you feel like worrying. It is love—a deep compassionate, heartfelt action verb—that pushes you to do the impossible for others! This is love.

Now take these definitions of love and compare it to Tina Turner's song "what's love got to do with it." *Listen.* I know you're saved now, but there was a time when you listened to songs like this. **An instant hit, the lyrics and delivery helped Tina become a household name.** Most of us know her story, but after leaving a man who was physically abusive, true definition of love became clear to her. In her words, "who needs a heart when a heart can be broken?" This song made all of us ask the fundamental questions, like *what is love, am I receiving real love, and how much does love matter in relationships?*

Chapter 22
Love according to 1 Corinthians 13

The truth is, love has everything to do with relationships. But the lie is that love is just about feelings, emotions, passion, and desire. Love is much bigger than how you feel today. Love, in a Christian context, is the only way to understand God. It is the fuel God gives us to relate to people. If your love definition is filled with fiction, everything else will fail. If you don't have love in check, you will forever be out of order. So, for those who think they know what love is, I invite you to erase your chalkboard, and look at what the Scripture tells us about love.

1 Corinthians 13:4-7
Love is patient, love is kind. It does not envy, it does not boast, it is not proud. It does not dishonor others, it is not self-seeking, it is not easily angered, it keeps no record of wrongs. Love does not delight in evil but rejoices with the truth. It always protects, always trusts, always hopes, always perseveres.

Whenever we are faced with the concept of love, we must differentiate the hallmark version of love from the Christ-like definition of love. The Hallmark version is filled with chocolate candy and hearts for Valentine's day.

The hallmark version promises poetry, fancy trips, walks on the beach, and front row tickets. Christ's love includes endurance, long-suffering, delayed gratification, patience and forgiveness. Christ's version doesn't always look as beautiful as Hallmark looks, but Christ's love is sure to last!

This is why it is important to know what the Scriptures say before you decide if you are in love! Whether you are praying about a spouse, a career, your ministry, or your purpose, go H.A.R.D. by loving hard. Learn how to cross-examine your desires with the Word of God. What does 1 Corinthians 13 say? First of all, love is patient. That means it waits until an infant grows up to become an adult. Love understands that people grow at different rates, and if it is going to be love, it must be patient enough to walk with people during their most immature seasons.

Love is also kind—this means, it doesn't express itself in an attitude of entitlement. It doesn't walk in the room expecting others to serve him. It gives an open and caring smile to everyone it meets. It cares for the brokenhearted and empathizes with the weak. It moves when others stand still. It goes where others won't go. Love honors and love promotes. Love doesn't take score and love doesn't gossip. All of those counter attitudes—gossip, backbiting, self-promotion, jealousy—are seeds from the fruit of fear. When you fear someone else's power, you downplay their value. When you fear what others can do to you, you never tell them "thank you." When those you are called to love intimidate you, you live a life of retaliation. You live a life of revenge. You want an eye for an eye, and the death penalty for the murderer. But this isn't love according to 1 Corinthians 13. God's love always takes the higher road. Even when friends let us down, we must take the high road. Even when bad things happen to us, and when we find ourselves alone, still we must take the highest road. Why? Because God is love, and since we call ourselves disciples, we must look like the God we promote. We cannot choose when we want to love God's way or when we want to love the "hallmark" way. Disciples who have decided to GO H.A.R.D. in their relationships have surrendered all to God. That means, we play by His rules. We have taken ourselves out of the will. And when we do that, God can truly be our potter again!

It was my wife who taught me how to love God's way. When we first got married, I thought I had it under control. I thought I knew how to love. Because I had been in relationships before, I figured I knew what I was doing. I wasn't afraid to say "I love you" and I knew what it was like to love someone through seasons of real pain. I was good at "agreeing to disagree." But marriage taught me something that no relationship before it could ever teach me. My first error was that I tried to make a permanent promise with a temporary permit. You know how we do—we promise not to say hurtful things for as long as we are together—then two weeks later, we catch ourselves saying hurtful things. That was my problem. I made a declaration that I wouldn't argue with my wife, and I wouldn't hurt her for as long as we were married. But I'm sure you know what happened. After 11+ years of blissful marriage, I've said many things that caused tears to fall from her eyes.

Like most men, I wrestled with talking about my feelings. I had a motto, "when I'm ready to talk, we will talk. But until then, let's keep it moving." But this wasn't love. This was control. I was only concerned about myself, and I didn't give much thought to my wife's needs and feelings.

The more I declared this motto, the more she hurt. Eventually, I perfected the technique of controlling the conversation, and many times, it would take weeks or months for us to converse. Imagine three months of hostility. Imagine three months of eating meals with a big elephant in the room. That's how I handled that relationship, until I realized that it wasn't working. She had become distant, and I had become indifferent.

If you're going to love the godly way, you must be willing to change what doesn't work. If she needs a hug, hug her. If he needs validation, validate him. Change what doesn't work, or what you don't change will never work for you. My method, at the time, was working for me because I didn't feel like talking, but the truth is, it was causing irreparable damage in my marriage. I didn't know it at the time, but many of my "old nature" characteristics were showing up in my marriage. Before Christ, I was selfish, over- confident, and prideful. Everybody, in my mind, could be replaced. Boy I was a hot mess! I was so full of pride. I didn't want to seem inferior by telling someone I needed them. So that is how I lived before Christ, and if we do not crucify our flesh daily and renew our mind in the world, we will drag our old habits and practices into our current situation. I had to do away with the "my way" mentality. In marriage, in life, and in love, life is about sacrificing for the one with whom you are in relationship. It is no longer your way. This is no longer your house, or your car, or your money—the language must change. The Bible says in 1 Corinthians 6:19 that we do not even belong to ourselves. It is this revelation, and the understanding of God as potter, that helped me to change the damaging love cycle in my life. Once I began to give God full permission to shape and reshape my life, my marriage started to change. I saw immediate changes in my wife's communication with me. Sometimes that is all it takes—a decision that allows God to mold you and make you in order to change the old nature into a new creature.

Chapter 23
Make A Change...Now!

What changes do you need to make? What can you do better? What big elephant are you ignoring in your relationships? I can't count the number of counseling sessions I've had with families who don't know how to be honest. They are sitting in my office, and they had no clue how they got into what they are into. Some of them are married, but they didn't marry for love. They know it was for lust. But now, they don't know how to fix the situation. Others got into bad relationships because they were lonely and needed to feel the comfort of someone else's presence.

I can recall a couple who was so "in love" that they skipped counseling just to get married quickly. If they had stayed for the first session, they would've heard me talk about the 3 kinds of love. Eros, Philos, and Agape. Eros love is erotic love, which is based on sight and infatuation. Philos is brotherly love, which means "I will do for you what you do for me." And then there is agape love, which is the greatest kind of love. It is unconditional love. It is the love of Jesus about which we spoke earlier. It gives of itself fully and doesn't expect a return for its actions.

Many people believe they have agape love, but they really have a mix between Eros and Philos. Agape love is for a lifetime. The other categories of love can be hindered by the struggles of life. Take for example the couple I mentioned a few moments ago. These two lovebirds were leading with their hearts, but their relationship had no connection to God. The woman loved the man's eyes, his broad shoulders, and she loved the way he treated her. The man loved everything about the woman, including her shape and her cooking. They were struggling financially, and both people lived in their respective parents' homes. When they came together, they decided to live with his parents. They got married, and a few months later, she got pregnant. From that moment, the relationship began to change. He wanted to go out more. She became more and more tired. He began to "do his thing" as if he wasn't married. Her life got busier and busier. Then the child came, and a few months later, she got pregnant again!

The man began to doubt if she was the one he was supposed to marry. The woman was crushed by this discovery and became depressed. Now she is broken. He is miserable. Life is a chore for her, and a slave ship to him. They sit at the dinner table in silence. What once was so attractive is now a nightmare. All because their love was not built on agape. God did not connect them—their emotions mislead them. Their problems increased as she tried to get child support. He stopped supporting his kids, but the courts denied her support because they were living under the same roof. She realized, sitting in a pool of tears, that her last ten years were led by heart decisions, not holy spirit decisions.

You may ask yourself "how could this happen?" Well, I will tell you. This happens because people don't pay attention to the details in the beginning. Like the impetuous people we are, humans are blinded by our wants, and we end up rolling downhill when we do not ask God to lead our love lives. For many of us, we don't realize how bad it has become until it is too late to turn around. But this doesn't have to be your story. You can defeat all odds and make some changes. First, you need to pray and confess your faults to a trusted mentor, pastor, or counselor. Next, you need to plan ways to confront the problem (in you) before you confront the problem in others. There are always two sides to every story, and you have to own up to the clues you missed along the way. God will redeem you and forgive you, but you've got to be willing to make some changes. If God frees you from a toxic relationship, stay out of it. Don't pull yourself back in because you miss "him," or because you "need one more night with her." Be sober, vigilant, and wise.

Going HARD will cause you to be uncomfortable sometimes, but if you only knew the bright destiny ahead of you, you would move past the good in order to pursue the greater! I beg you, reader, to make the necessary changes to grow. Ask God for the strategy to move forward, and the grace to forgive those who have done you wrong. No matter how difficult it seems right now, God is able to turn your entire life around.

Acknowledgements

Thank you, Lord for the experiences that have created the content for this book; for every moment that caused a road block, obstacle, or impediment you have helped me overcome. Without the Lord this and everything to follow would not be possible. To my wife and best friend, my lady Traci Akins; you are my destiny partner and a continual wind beneath my wings that allow me to soar. You inspire me every day to work hard at being a better husband, father & man I love you.

To My children Nia & Nehemiah watching you grow has caused me to push and GO HARD in life so you can have a model to look after. You are my greatest legacy of love. I pray your success is released through your faith in God and your ability to see His greatness inside of you. You both have sacrificed, and I thank you. To Tyree, my son you have grown to see that a Go Hard mentality is necessary for your success. I pray that all you see in me, you will take every good thing and use it to release faith in your life. I love you as my own seed!

To my Brother, Joshua, thank you for you love, your Go Hard mentality to become a Police officer, Airborne trooper and pressing to the mark and to my mother and father Pam & Fred Jenkins, thank you for your guidance, prayers & paying for college so I wouldn't be in debt. I appreciate your example dad as a servant and how you serve others. Mom you are phenomenal in every way.

You've inspired me to get up early and be productive.

To my spiritual leader Bishop Vaughn McLauglin, thank you for being the extraordinary man with wisdom and care. if it was not for you I would have listen to God when he told me to step out. You have encouraged me every Wednesday and you keep pushing causing everyone around you to keep pushing. Thank you again.
To what I would consider my natural Father in the gospel, Bishop Donald Hilliard, thanking you may not hold enough weight to the gratitude I have towards, you raised me under the blood stain banner of walking holy. I owe who I am because I watched you as a young man serve the Lord. Thank you for being an author, pastor, father & great leader.

To my natural family and Triumphant life family each of you have been such a great support. Thank you for trusting me to practice on you, before sharing my vision to the world. I love serving you through teaching, preaching, counseling, and being the prophetic voice in your life, thanks. I am honored that God would trust me with you.

To Greg & Ida Hopson; you both have been like solid ground beneath my feet. This book is a reality because of your pushing and encouraging me to finish, thank you. Thank you for sticking with me through ups and downs. You both are awesome. I Love you both.

To Godzchild, Shaun & Ana, thank you for putting it all together and making it look right, sound right and all that you guys do to aid people in becoming the author that's trapped on the inside.

Akins Ministry
500 Malterer Avenue, Oceanport NJ 07757
www.relationshipsuniversity.com

www.ingramcontent.com/pod-product-compliance
Lightning Source LLC
Chambersburg PA
CBHW052202110526
44591CB00012B/2045